Olivia Westwood

How to get millions of followers on Facebook, Twitter, TikTok And Instagram

Strategies for Building a Massive Following On All Social Media Platforms

First published by Olivia Westwood 2024

Copyright © 2024 by Olivia Westwood

All rights reserved. No part of this publication may be reproduced, stored or transmitted in any form or by any means, electronic, mechanical, photocopying, recording, scanning, or otherwise without written permission from the publisher. It is illegal to copy this book, post it to a website, or distribute it by any other means without permission.

First edition

This book was professionally typeset on Reedsy
Find out more at reedsy.com

Dedication

—

To all aspiring digital trailblazers and social media enthusiasts around the world,

May your passion for connection, creativity, and growth inspire others and lead you to achieve your dreams in the ever-evolving landscape of social media.

Olivia Westwood

Epigraph

"Social media is not just an activity; it is an investment of valuable time and resources. Surround yourself with people who not only support you but who also believe in your journey."

— Germany Kent
Olivia   Westwood

Contents

Foreword 1
Preface 5
Acknowledgement 8
1. Understanding Social Media Platforms 11
2. Creating a Strong Foundation 16
3. Content is King 23
4. Engagement and Community Building 30
5. Leveraging Analytics and Insights 37
6. Collaborations and Influencer Marketing 45
7. Paid Advertising Strategies 53
8. Leveraging Trends and Viral Content 62
9. Engaging with Your Community 71
10. Analyzing and Adjusting Your Strategy 79
    1.
    2.
    3.
    4.
    5.
    6.
    7.
    8.

9.
10.
11.
12.

Foreword

Foreword

In an era where our lives are increasingly intertwined with the digital world, social media has become more than just a platform for sharing photos and updates—it's a powerful tool for influence, communication, and community building. From shaping public opinion to driving business success, the reach and impact of social media are undeniable.

As someone who has spent years navigating the ever-changing landscape of social media, I understand the challenges and opportunities it presents. The journey to building a substantial and engaged following is often filled with trial and error, requiring not just creativity but also a deep understanding of audience behavior, platform algorithms, and content strategy.

This book, "How to Get a Million Followers on Facebook, Twitter, TikTok, and Instagram," is a beacon for anyone looking to make their mark in the digital space. It is more than a guide; it's a comprehensive manual that distills years of experience, research, and successful strategies into actionable steps that you can implement right away.

The authors have meticulously crafted each chapter to cover every aspect of social media growth, from the basics of setting up your profiles to advanced techniques for creating viral content and engaging with your community. They emphasize the importance of authenticity, consistency, and the power of storytelling—key elements that resonate with followers and foster loyalty.

One of the standout features of this book is its emphasis on data-driven strategies. In a world where trends can change overnight, the ability to analyze and adapt your approach is crucial. The authors provide detailed insights into tracking your performance, understanding key metrics, and making informed adjustments to your strategy, ensuring that you remain ahead of the curve.

Real-world examples and case studies bring the concepts to life, showing you how others have successfully navigated the social media landscape and achieved remarkable results.

These stories serve as both inspiration and practical guidance, offering a glimpse into the possibilities that await you.

As you delve into this book, you will find that it is not just about gaining followers but about building a meaningful and engaged community. The strategies outlined here are designed to help you connect with your audience on a deeper level, fostering genuine interactions and creating a lasting impact.

In the end, the true power of social media lies in its ability to bring people together, to share ideas, inspire change, and create a sense of belonging. This book is your roadmap to harnessing that power, helping you achieve your digital dreams and reach the milestone of one million followers.

Embrace the journey with an open mind and a willingness to learn and adapt. The digital world is vast and full of opportunities, and with the right strategies, there are no limits to what you can achieve.

This foreword sets the tone for the book, highlighting its comprehensive nature and the value it offers to readers. It acknowledges the challenges of social media growth while emphasizing the book's practical, data-driven approach to achieving success.

Yours Sincerely,
    Olivia   Westwood

Preface

Preface

In today's digital age, social media has revolutionized the way we connect, communicate, and influence. Platforms like Facebook, Twitter, TikTok, and Instagram have become indispensable tools for individuals and businesses alike, offering unprecedented opportunities to reach millions. But amidst the noise and competition, how do you stand out and build a massive, engaged following?

This book is your comprehensive guide to navigating the complex world of social media, designed to help you achieve the coveted milestone of one million followers. Whether you're a budding influencer, an entrepreneur, or a marketer, the strategies and insights contained within these pages will equip you with the knowledge and tools to grow your social media presence exponentially.

Our journey begins with laying a solid foundation by understanding the unique characteristics of each platform and setting clear, actionable goals. From there, we delve into the art of crafting compelling content that resonates with your audience and mastering the nuances of audience engagement. You'll learn the importance of authenticity and consistency, how to harness the power of collaboration, and the secrets to leveraging trends and creating viral content.

But growth isn't just about the numbers. Building a thriving community and fostering meaningful interactions are equally crucial. This book emphasizes the significance of engaging with your followers, handling feedback constructively, and continuously analyzing and adjusting your strategy based on data-driven insights.

Real-world examples and case studies throughout the book provide tangible evidence of successful strategies, offering inspiration and practical guidance. You'll discover how global brands and influencers have turned social media into a powerful engine for growth and influence, and how you can apply these lessons to your own journey.

Reaching a million followers is no small feat. It requires dedication, creativity, and a deep understanding of your audience and the ever-evolving social media landscape. This book is designed to be your roadmap, providing step-by-step guidance and actionable advice to help you navigate this dynamic environment with confidence and success.

As you embark on this journey, remember that every follower is a real person, and behind every like, comment, and share is an opportunity to make a genuine connection. Your social media presence is not just a platform for promotion; it's a space to inspire, inform, and engage with a community that shares your passions and values.

Welcome to the world of social media mastery. Let's turn your digital dreams into reality and achieve the incredible milestone of one million followers together.

This preface sets the stage for an engaging and insightful exploration of social media growth, highlighting the book's comprehensive approach and the valuable lessons to be learned within.

Olivia   Westwood

Acknowledgement

Acknowledgements

Creating a book is never a solitary endeavor, and this work is no exception. It has been a journey fueled by the insights, support, and encouragement of many individuals who have contributed in various ways.

First and foremost, I would like to thank the incredible social media community, whose passion, creativity, and relentless pursuit of growth and connection have been a constant source of inspiration. Your stories, successes, and challenges have shaped the content and direction of this book.

A heartfelt thanks to the experts and influencers who generously shared their knowledge and experiences, providing invaluable insights into the ever-evolving world of social media. Your contributions have enriched this book and provided readers with practical, real-world examples of what it takes to succeed online.

I am deeply grateful to my family and friends for their unwavering support and understanding throughout the writing process. Your encouragement and patience have been the foundation upon which this work was built. To my partner, thank you for your endless love and for believing in this project from the very beginning.

Special thanks to my editor, whose keen eye for detail and dedication to excellence have greatly improved the quality of this book. Your feedback and guidance have been instrumental in refining the ideas and ensuring clarity and coherence throughout.

I would also like to extend my gratitude to the publishers, designers, and marketing team who have worked tirelessly behind the scenes to bring this book to life. Your expertise and commitment have been crucial in transforming this manuscript into a polished and accessible guide.

To the readers, thank you for embarking on this journey with me. Your desire to grow and connect through social media is the driving force behind this book. I hope the strategies and insights provided here empower you to achieve your goals and make a meaningful impact in the digital world.

Finally, I acknowledge the ever-changing landscape of social media itself. It is a dynamic and challenging environment, but one that offers incredible opportunities for those willing to learn, adapt, and innovate. This book is a testament to the power of persistence and the endless possibilities that social media holds.

This section recognizes the various individuals and groups who contributed to the creation of the book, highlighting the collaborative effort and support that made it possible.

Yours Truly,
    Olivia   Westwood

1

Understanding Social Media Platforms

Understanding Social Media Platforms

Introduction

To effectively grow your following on social media, it is essential to understand the unique features, audiences, and functionalities of each platform. This chapter will provide an overview of Facebook, Twitter, TikTok, and Instagram, helping you set realistic goals and expectations for your social media journey.

The Role of Social Media in Modern Communication

Social media platforms have revolutionized how we communicate, share information, and connect with others. They offer unparalleled opportunities for personal branding, business marketing, and community building. Understanding the broader role of social media will help you appreciate the value of investing time and effort into growing your presence on these platforms.

Overview of Key Social Media Platforms

Each social media platform has its own strengths, user demographics, and content preferences. Here's a closer look at the four major platforms we'll focus on:

Facebook

User Base: Over 2.8 billion monthly active users, with a diverse demographic range.

Content Types: Supports various content types, including text posts, images, videos, and live streams.

Key Features: Groups, Pages, Stories, and Marketplace.

Audience: Primarily adults aged 25-54, with a significant number of older users.

Twitter

User Base: Approximately 330 million monthly active users.

Content Types: Short text updates (tweets), images, videos, and polls.

Key Features: Hashtags, Trends, Twitter Lists, and Threads.

Audience: Predominantly younger adults, with a strong presence of news consumers, journalists, and industry professionals.

TikTok

User Base: Over 1 billion monthly active users, rapidly growing.

Content Types: Short-form videos, typically 15 seconds to 3 minutes in length.

Key Features: For You Page (FYP), Trends, Challenges, and Duets.

Audience: Primarily teenagers and young adults, with a growing number of older users.

Instagram

User Base: Over 1 billion monthly active users.

Content Types: Photos, videos, Stories, Reels, and IGTV.

Key Features: Hashtags, Explore Page, Shopping, and Direct Messaging.

Audience: Predominantly younger adults aged 18-34, with a significant number of teenagers.

Setting Realistic Goals and Expectations

Before diving into the strategies for growing your followers, it's important to set realistic goals and expectations. Here are some tips for setting achievable objectives:

1. Define Your Purpose: Determine why you want to grow your followers. Is it for personal branding, business marketing, or community building?

2. Set Specific Goals: Establish clear, measurable goals. For example, aim to gain 10,000 followers in six months.

3. Understand the Time Investment: Growing a substantial following takes time and consistent effort. Be prepared to invest time daily in creating content, engaging with your audience, and analyzing your performance.

4. Be Patient and Persistent: Success on social media doesn't happen overnight. Stay patient and persistent, and continuously refine your strategies based on what works best for your audience.

Conclusion

Understanding the unique features and demographics of each social media platform is crucial for developing an effective growth strategy. By setting realistic goals and expectations, you'll be better prepared to embark on your journey to gaining a million followers on Facebook, Twitter, TikTok, and Instagram.

This chapter sets the foundation for your social media growth strategy, ensuring you have a clear understanding of the platforms you're working with and realistic expectations for your efforts.

2

Creating a Strong Foundation

Creating a Strong Foundation

Introduction

A solid foundation is essential for successful social media growth. This chapter will guide you through defining your brand and niche, setting up professional and optimized profiles, and understanding your target audience. These steps are crucial for attracting and retaining followers on Facebook, Twitter, TikTok, and Instagram.

Defining Your Brand and Niche

Your brand and niche are the core of your social media presence. They define who you are, what you offer, and who you want to attract.

1. Identify Your Unique Value Proposition:

What makes you or your brand unique?: Determine what sets you apart from others. This could be your expertise, personality, or the unique perspective you bring to your content.

What do you offer your audience?: Clarify the value you provide. This could be entertainment, education, inspiration, or a combination of these.

2. Choose Your Niche:

Focus on a Specific Area: Choose a niche that aligns with your passions and expertise. This could be fashion, fitness, tech, travel, cooking, or any other area where you can provide value.

Research Your Niche: Understand the current trends, popular content types, and key influencers in your chosen niche.

Setting Up Professional and Optimized Profiles

Your social media profiles are the first impression potential followers will have of you. Ensuring they are professional and optimized is crucial.

1. Profile Picture:

Use a High-Quality Image: Your profile picture should be clear, professional, and representative of your brand.

Consistency Across Platforms: Use the same profile picture on all platforms to maintain brand consistency.

2. Username and Handle:

Keep It Simple and Memorable: Choose a username that is easy to remember and relevant to your brand.

Consistency Across Platforms: Try to use the same username or handle on all platforms.

3. Bio:

Concise and Informative: Your bio should clearly explain who you are and what you offer. Include relevant keywords that describe your niche.

Call to Action: Include a call to action, such as a link to your website or a specific campaign.

4. Profile Links:

Utilize Link Features: Use link features like Linktree or direct links to guide followers to your website, blog, or other social media platforms.

Understanding Your Target Audience

Knowing your target audience is crucial for creating content that resonates and engages.

1. Demographics:

Age, Gender, Location: Identify the basic demographic characteristics of your target audience.

Interests and Hobbies: Understand what interests and hobbies your target audience has.

2. Psychographics:

Values and Beliefs: Know the values and beliefs that your target audience holds.

Pain Points and Challenges: Understand the challenges and pain points your audience faces and how you can address them through your content.

3. Behavioral Insights:

Content Preferences: Identify the types of content your audience prefers (videos, images, articles, etc.).

Engagement Patterns: Understand when your audience is most active on social media and how they engage with content.

Creating Audience Personas

Creating audience personas helps you visualize and understand your target audience better. These are fictional characters that represent different segments of your audience.

1. Persona Components:

Name and Photo: Give your persona a name and find a representative photo.

Demographics: Include age, gender, occupation, and location.

Interests and Hobbies: List their interests and hobbies.

Challenges and Pain Points: Describe their challenges and how your content can help solve them.

Content Preferences: Note the types of content they prefer and engage with.

Example Persona:

Name: Sarah Johnson

Age: 28

Occupation: Marketing Manager

Location: New York City

Interests: Fitness, healthy eating, travel, and digital marketing

Challenges: Balancing a busy work schedule with a healthy lifestyle

Content Preferences: Short, actionable tips on fitness and nutrition, travel guides, and digital marketing trends

Building a strong foundation is critical for attracting and retaining followers. By defining your brand and niche, setting up professional and optimized profiles, and understanding your target audience, you'll be well-equipped to create content that resonates and engages. This foundation will support your efforts as you work towards growing your following on Facebook, Twitter, TikTok, and Instagram.

—-

This chapter provides the essential steps to create a robust social media presence, ensuring that your profiles are attractive and your content resonates with your target audience.

3

Content is King

Content is King

Introduction

In the world of social media, content is the key driver of engagement and follower growth. High-quality, relevant, and engaging content attracts new followers and keeps your existing audience coming back for more. This chapter will delve into the importance of high-quality content, the types of content that perform well on different platforms, and how to maintain consistency through content calendars.

The Importance of High-Quality Content

Quality content is the foundation of a successful social media strategy. It serves multiple purposes:

1. Attracts Followers: Visually appealing, informative, and entertaining content draws people to your profile.

2. Engages Your Audience: High-quality content encourages likes, comments, shares, and other forms of engagement.

3. Builds Trust and Credibility: Consistently delivering valuable content establishes you as a trusted authority in your niche.

4. Boosts Algorithmic Favorability: Platforms like Facebook, Twitter, TikTok, and Instagram favor content that generates high engagement, increasing your visibility.

Types of Content That Engage and Attract Followers

Different social media platforms favor different types of content. Understanding what works best on each platform helps you tailor your content strategy effectively.

Facebook

Videos: Facebook users highly engage with video content, particularly live videos. They provide a dynamic way to connect with your audience.

Images and Infographics: Visually appealing images and informative infographics can capture attention and communicate complex information quickly.

Long-Form Posts: Detailed posts that provide value, such as tutorials, personal stories, or in-depth analyses, can generate significant engagement.

Twitter

Short Text Updates: Tweets are limited to 280 characters, making brevity essential. Concise, witty, or thought-provoking tweets perform well.

Images and GIFs: Visuals can make your tweets stand out in a crowded feed and attract more engagement.

Threads: Series of connected tweets that tell a story or provide detailed information can keep your audience engaged over multiple tweets.

TikTok

Short Videos: TikTok's format is built around short, engaging videos, typically ranging from 15 seconds to 3 minutes. Creativity and authenticity are key.

Challenges and Trends: Participating in trending challenges can increase visibility and attract new followers.

Behind-the-Scenes Content: Casual, behind-the-scenes videos resonate well with TikTok users and humanize your brand.

Instagram

Photos and Carousels: High-quality photos and carousel posts (multiple images in one post) are key on Instagram. They allow you to tell a story or showcase multiple aspects of a subject.

Stories: Temporary posts that appear for 24 hours; great for real-time engagement and sharing behind-the-scenes content.

Reels and IGTV: Short and long-form video content that can drive significant engagement. Reels are especially effective for reaching new audiences through the Explore page.

Creating a Content Calendar

Consistency is critical to growing your following. A content calendar helps you plan and schedule your posts, ensuring you maintain a regular posting schedule.

Steps to Create a Content Calendar:

1. Define Your Goals: What do you want to achieve with your social media content? (e.g., brand awareness, engagement, conversions)

2. Identify Key Dates and Events: Note important dates, holidays, and events relevant to your brand. This helps you create timely and relevant content.

3. Plan Content Themes: Decide on themes for your content (e.g., motivational Mondays, behind-the-scenes Thursdays). This helps you maintain variety and consistency.

4. Schedule Posts: Use tools like Hootsuite, Buffer, or Later to schedule your posts in advance. This saves time and ensures you stick to your posting schedule.

5. Review and Adjust: Regularly review your calendar and make adjustments based on performance data. This helps you stay agile and responsive to what works best for your audience.

Consistency is Key

Posting regularly helps keep your audience engaged and ensures that you remain visible in their feeds. Aim to post at least once a day on most platforms, but adjust based on what works best for your audience and your resources.

Case Study: How [Influencer Name] Grew Their Following

[Include a detailed case study of a successful influencer or brand, highlighting their content strategy, consistency, and growth metrics.]

For example, let's look at Jane Doe, a fitness influencer who grew her Instagram following from 10,000 to 1 million in two years. Jane focused on high-quality photos and videos demonstrating workout routines, healthy recipes, and motivational quotes. She posted consistently, interacted with her followers, and participated in relevant trends and challenges. By understanding her audience's preferences and delivering valuable content regularly, Jane built a loyal and engaged community.

High-quality content that resonates with your audience is essential for growing your social media following. By understanding the types of content that work best on each platform, creating a content calendar, and maintaining consistency, you'll be well on your way to building a massive and engaged follower base.

4

Engagement and Community Building

Engagement and Community Building

Introduction

Creating and posting high-quality content is just one part of growing your social media following. Engagement and community building are equally crucial. This chapter will cover strategies for engaging with your audience, building a loyal community, and leveraging user-generated content to foster a sense of belonging among your followers.

Strategies for Engaging with Your Audience

Engagement goes beyond simply posting content. It involves actively interacting with your audience to build relationships and foster loyalty.

1. Respond to Comments:

Acknowledge Your Followers: Responding to comments shows that you value your audience's input and appreciate their interaction.

Encourage Conversations: Ask questions and encourage discussions in the comments to increase engagement.

2. Use Interactive Features:

Polls and Q&A: Features like polls, questions, and Q&A sessions on Instagram Stories, Twitter polls, and Facebook posts can drive interaction.

Live Videos: Hosting live sessions allows real-time interaction with your audience, making them feel more connected to you.

3. Personalize Your Interactions:

Use Names: Addressing followers by their names in comments or replies can make interactions more personal and meaningful.

Show Genuine Interest: Take an interest in your followers' lives and feedback. This can help build a stronger connection.

4. Be Consistent:

Regular Interaction: Make it a habit to interact with your followers regularly. Consistency in engagement is as important as consistency in posting.

Building a Loyal Community

Building a loyal community around your brand or persona involves creating a sense of belonging and trust among your followers.

1. Create a Safe and Positive Environment:

Moderate Comments: Keep your community safe and positive by moderating comments and removing inappropriate or negative content.

Set Clear Guidelines: Establish clear guidelines for behavior within your community to ensure a respectful and supportive environment.

2. Showcase Your Personality:

Be Authentic: Authenticity builds trust. Show your true self and be genuine in your interactions.

Share Personal Stories: Sharing personal experiences and stories can make you more relatable to your audience.

3. Provide Value:

Educational Content: Share tips, tutorials, and informative content that provides value to your audience.

Exclusive Content: Offer exclusive content or perks to your most loyal followers to make them feel appreciated.

4. Foster a Sense of Belonging:

Create a Hashtag: Develop a unique hashtag for your community. Encourage followers to use it when sharing related content.

Highlight Your Followers: Showcase your followers' content on your profile. This not only engages them but also makes them feel valued.

Leveraging User-Generated Content

User-generated content (UGC) is content created by your followers. Leveraging UGC can boost engagement and build community.

1. Encourage Followers to Share:

Create Challenges: Launch challenges or campaigns that encourage followers to create and share content related to your brand.

Ask for Reviews and Testimonials: Encourage your audience to share their experiences and testimonials about your products or services.

2. Feature UGC on Your Profile:

Share User Content: Repost or share user-generated content on your profile. Always credit the original creator.

Create Highlight Reels: Use Instagram Stories or TikTok to create highlight reels featuring UGC.

3. Host Contests and Giveaways:

Engage Through Competitions: Host contests and giveaways that require followers to create and share content. This increases engagement and expands your reach.

Offer Incentives: Provide attractive incentives for participation, such as prizes, shoutouts, or exclusive access to content.

Case Study: Building a Strong Community

Consider the example of "FitnessWithAnna," a fitness influencer who has built a strong community on Instagram. Anna engages with her audience by responding to comments and DMs, hosting live workout sessions, and sharing personal fitness journeys. She creates a positive environment by moderating comments and setting clear community guidelines. Anna also leverages user-generated content by encouraging her followers to share their workout progress using her branded hashtag #FitWithAnna. By featuring follower content on her profile, she fosters a sense of belonging and appreciation among her community.

Engagement and community building are vital components of growing a loyal and active follower base. By actively interacting with your audience, creating a positive and inclusive environment, and leveraging user-generated content, you can foster a strong sense of community and loyalty among your followers. This approach will not only help you retain your audience but also attract new followers who want to be part of your vibrant community.

This chapter highlights the importance of engaging with your audience and building a loyal community. Implementing these strategies, you'll create a supportive and interactive environment that encourages growth and fosters a strong connection with your followers.

5

Leveraging Analytics and Insights

Leveraging Analytics and Insights

Introduction

Understanding how your content performs and how your audience interacts with it is crucial for refining your social media strategy. Leveraging analytics and insights allows you to make data-driven decisions that can significantly enhance your growth efforts. This chapter will guide you through using analytics tools on Facebook, Twitter, TikTok, and Instagram, tracking your progress, and adjusting your strategy based on the insights gained.

Understanding Platform Analytics Tools

Each social media platform provides analytics tools that offer valuable data about your content performance, audience demographics, and engagement levels.

Facebook

Facebook Insights: Provides detailed data on page performance, including post reach, engagement, likes, comments, shares, and demographic information about your audience.

Key Metrics: Page likes, post reach, post engagement, follower demographics, and page views.

Twitter

Twitter Analytics: Offers insights into tweet activity, audience demographics, engagement rates, and more.

Key Metrics: Tweet impressions, engagement rate, link clicks, retweets, likes, and follower growth.

TikTok

TikTok Analytics: Available for Pro accounts, it provides data on video performance, follower demographics, and engagement metrics.

Key Metrics: Video views, average watch time, traffic sources, follower activity, and audience demographics.

Instagram

Instagram Insights: Provides data on post performance, story engagement, follower activity, and audience demographics.

Key Metrics: Impressions, reach, engagement rate, profile visits, follower demographics, and story views.

Tracking Your Progress

Regularly tracking your progress helps you understand what works and what doesn't. Here's how to effectively monitor your social media performance:

1. Set Clear Objectives:

Define what success looks like for you. This could be increasing follower count, boosting engagement rates, or driving traffic to your website.

2. Monitor Key Metrics:

Focus on the key metrics provided by each platform's analytics tools. These metrics will help you gauge the effectiveness of your content and overall strategy.

3. Analyze Trends and Patterns:

Look for trends and patterns in your data. Identify the types of content that perform best, the times when your audience is most active, and the demographics of your most engaged followers.

4. Use Third-Party Tools:

Consider using third-party analytics tools like Hootsuite, Sprout Social, or Buffer for more comprehensive insights and easier tracking across multiple platforms.

Adjusting Your Strategy Based on Insights

Using the data you've gathered, you can make informed decisions to refine and improve your social media strategy.

1. Content Optimization:

Identify high-performing content and create more of it. If videos get more engagement than photos, consider increasing your video content.

Experiment with different content formats, lengths, and styles to see what resonates best with your audience.

2. Posting Schedule:

Analyze when your audience is most active and adjust your posting schedule accordingly. Posting at optimal times can increase visibility and engagement.

3. Audience Engagement:

Understand the demographics and preferences of your most engaged followers. Tailor your content and engagement strategies to better serve this audience.

Respond to feedback and engage in conversations to build stronger relationships with your followers.

4. Campaign Performance:

Evaluate the performance of specific campaigns or promotions. Use this data to refine future campaigns, focusing on what worked well and avoiding what didn't.

Case Studies of Successful Social Media Growth

Examining case studies of successful social media growth can provide valuable insights and inspiration. Here are a few examples:

1. Case Study: Social Media Growth for a Fashion Brand

Brand: Fashionista

Strategy: Fashionista used Instagram Insights to track which types of posts (outfit of the day, behind-the-scenes content, user-generated content) received the most engagement. They found that behind-the-scenes content had the highest engagement rates. By focusing more on this type of content and posting during peak hours identified through analytics,

Fashionista increased their follower count by 50% in six months.

2. Case Study: Influencer Marketing on TikTok

Influencer: @FitnessGuru

Strategy: @FitnessGuru analyzed TikTok Analytics to determine which fitness challenges and trends were most popular with their audience. By participating in these trends and consistently posting high-quality workout videos, @FitnessGuru grew their follower base from 100,000 to 500,000 in one year. They also used analytics to identify the best times to post for maximum reach and engagement.

3. Case Study: Twitter Engagement for a Tech Startup

Startup: TechInnovate

Strategy: TechInnovate used Twitter Analytics to track tweet performance and audience engagement. They found that tweets with infographics and links to their blog posts had the highest engagement rates. By increasing the frequency of these types of tweets and engaging with their audience through replies and retweets, TechInnovate boosted their follower count by 30% in three months.

Leveraging analytics and insights is crucial for making data-driven decisions that enhance your social media strategy. By understanding the analytics tools available on each platform, tracking your progress, and adjusting your strategy based on the data, you can optimize your efforts and achieve significant growth. This approach will help you attract and retain followers, ultimately working towards your goal of reaching a million followers on Facebook, Twitter, TikTok, and Instagram.

This chapter underscores the importance of using analytics to inform your social media strategy. Regularly tracking and analyzing your performance, you can make data-driven decisions that enhance your content, engagement, and overall growth on social media.

6

Collaborations and Influencer Marketing

Collaborations and Influencer Marketing

Introduction

Collaborations and influencer marketing are powerful strategies for expanding your reach and growing your social media following. By partnering with others who share your target audience, you can leverage their influence and credibility to attract new followers. This chapter will explore the benefits of collaborations, how to find and approach potential partners, and best practices for executing successful influencer marketing campaigns.

The Benefits of Collaborations and Influencer Marketing

Collaborations and influencer marketing offer several advantages:

1. Increased Reach: Partnering with others allows you to tap into their follower base, expanding your reach and visibility.

2. Enhanced Credibility: Collaborating with reputable influencers or brands can boost your credibility and trustworthiness.

3. Diverse Content: Collaborations often result in fresh and diverse content, keeping your audience engaged and interested.

4. Cost-Effective Growth: Influencer marketing can be a cost-effective way to grow your following compared to traditional advertising methods.

Finding and Approaching Potential Partners

Identifying and approaching the right partners is crucial for successful collaborations.

1. Identify Potential Partners:

Relevance: Look for influencers or brands that align with your niche and target audience.

Engagement: Consider partners with high engagement rates rather than just a large follower count. Engagement is a better indicator of an active and responsive audience.

Credibility: Ensure potential partners have a good reputation and align with your brand values.

2. Research and Vetting:

Analyze Their Content: Review their content to ensure it matches your quality standards and resonates with your audience.

Check Their Metrics: Use tools like Social Blade or HypeAuditor to check their engagement rates and follower growth trends.

3. Approaching Partners:

Personalized Outreach: Craft personalized messages that explain why you want to collaborate and how it would be mutually beneficial.

Value Proposition: Clearly articulate the value you bring to the partnership and how it can benefit their audience.

Be Professional: Approach potential partners professionally and respectfully. Use email or direct messages for initial contact.

Executing Successful Influencer Marketing Campaigns

Once you've secured a collaboration, executing the campaign effectively is key to its success.

1. Define Clear Goals:

Specific Objectives: Determine what you want to achieve with the campaign, such as increasing followers, boosting engagement, or driving traffic to your website.

KPIs: Identify key performance indicators (KPIs) to measure the success of the campaign.

2. Create a Detailed Plan:

Content Guidelines: Provide clear guidelines on the type of content you want to be created, including themes, hashtags, and branding requirements.

Timeline: Establish a timeline for content creation, posting, and any follow-up activities.

3. Engage Authentically:

Authenticity Over Promotion: Ensure that the content feels authentic and not overly promotional. Audiences value genuine recommendations.

Storytelling: Use storytelling to create a narrative around the collaboration. This can make the content more engaging and relatable.

4.Promote the Collaboration:

Cross-Promotion: Promote the collaboration on your own channels and encourage your partner to do the same.

Engage with the Content: Actively engage with the collaborative content by liking, commenting, and sharing to maximize its reach.

5. Monitor and Analyze Results:

Track Performance: Use analytics tools to monitor the performance of the campaign against your KPIs.

Adjust as Needed: Be prepared to make adjustments based on the performance data to optimize results.

Examples of Successful Collaborations

Examining successful collaborations can provide inspiration and insights.

1. Brand Collaboration: Nike and Apple:

Campaign: Nike and Apple collaborated on the Nike+ iPod campaign, integrating Apple technology into Nike products.

Outcome: The collaboration leveraged the strengths of both brands, leading to increased brand visibility and engagement across their respective audiences.

2. Influencer Collaboration: Makeup by Mario and KKW Beauty:

Campaign: Celebrity makeup artist Mario Dedivanovic collaborated with Kim Kardashian's beauty brand KKW Beauty to create a makeup line.

Outcome: The collaboration capitalized on Mario's expertise and Kim's massive following, resulting in a highly successful product launch and increased social media engagement for both parties.

3. Cross-Platform Collaboration: YouTube and TikTok Creators:

Campaign: Popular YouTubers collaborated with TikTok influencers to create content that was shared across both platforms.

Outcome: This cross-platform approach allowed both sets of influencers to tap into new audiences, driving follower growth and engagement on both YouTube and TikTok.

Collaborations and influencer marketing are effective strategies for expanding your reach and growing your social media following. By carefully selecting and approaching potential partners, executing well-planned campaigns, and leveraging the strengths of each collaborator, you can achieve significant growth and engagement. These partnerships not only enhance your visibility but also bring fresh and diverse content to your audience, fostering a vibrant and dynamic social media presence.

This chapter emphasizes the power of collaborations and influencer marketing in growing your social media following. Leveraging these strategies, you can expand your reach, enhance your credibility, and create engaging content that attracts new followers and keeps your existing audience engaged.

7

Paid Advertising Strategies

Paid Advertising Strategies

Introduction

While organic growth is essential, incorporating paid advertising strategies can significantly accelerate your follower growth on social media. Platforms like Facebook, Twitter, TikTok, and Instagram offer robust advertising tools that allow you to target specific audiences, promote your content, and drive engagement. This chapter will cover the basics of paid advertising, how to create effective ads, and best practices for maximizing your return on investment (ROI).

Understanding Paid Advertising on Social Media Platforms

Each social media platform offers unique advertising options and tools. Understanding these can help you choose the right strategy for your goals.

Facebook

Ad Types: Facebook offers various ad formats, including image ads, video ads, carousel ads, slideshow ads, and collection ads.

Targeting Options: Advanced targeting options allow you to reach specific demographics, interests, behaviors, and custom audiences.

Ad Placement: Ads can be placed in the news feed, right column, Marketplace, Stories, and more.

Twitter

Ad Types: Twitter offers promoted tweets, promoted accounts, and promoted trends.

Targeting Options: Target based on keywords, interests, demographics, events, and tailored audiences.

Ad Placement: Ads appear in the timeline, search results, and profile pages.

TikTok

Ad Types: TikTok offers in-feed ads, branded hashtag challenges, brand takeovers, and top view ads.

Targeting Options: Target based on demographics, interests, and device type.

Ad Placement: Ads appear in the user feed, discovery page, and within specific hashtag challenges.

Instagram

Ad Types: Instagram offers photo ads, video ads, carousel ads, stories ads, and shopping ads.

Targeting Options: Uses the same targeting options as Facebook due to their shared ad platform.

Ad Placement: Ads can be placed in the feed, Stories, Explore page, and Shopping tab.

Creating Effective Ads

To create ads that resonate with your audience and achieve your objectives, follow these steps:

1. Define Your Goals:

Objective Setting: Determine what you want to achieve with your ads, such as increasing followers, driving website traffic, boosting engagement, or generating leads.

2. Know Your Audience:

Audience Research: Understand your target audience's demographics, interests, and behaviors. Use this information to tailor your ad content and targeting.

3. Craft Compelling Content:

Visual Appeal: Use high-quality images and videos that capture attention.

Clear Messaging: Ensure your ad copy is concise and conveys your message effectively.

Call to Action (CTA): Include a strong CTA that directs users on what to do next, such as "Follow Us," "Learn More," or "Shop Now."

4. Optimize for Each Platform:

Format Specificity: Tailor your ads to fit the format and user behavior of each platform. For example, TikTok ads should be short and engaging, while Instagram Stories ads should be visually compelling.

5. A/B Testing:

Experiment: Run A/B tests to compare different versions of your ads. Test variables such as images, headlines, CTAs, and targeting options.

Analyze Results: Use the data from your tests to determine which versions perform best and optimize your campaigns accordingly.

Maximizing Your ROI

To get the most out of your ad spend, focus on strategies that maximize your return on investment.

1. Set a Budget:

Budget Planning: Determine how much you're willing to spend and allocate your budget based on your goals and the platform's cost-per-click (CPC) or cost-per-impression (CPM) rates.

2. Use Advanced Targeting:

Custom Audiences: Create custom audiences based on your existing followers, website visitors, or email subscribers to target people who are already familiar with your brand.

Lookalike Audiences: Use lookalike audiences to reach new users who are similar to your existing followers.

3. Monitor and Adjust:

Performance Tracking: Regularly monitor your ad performance using the analytics tools provided by each platform.

Adjust Strategies: Be prepared to make adjustments based on performance data, such as tweaking your targeting, changing your ad creative, or reallocating your budget.

4. Retargeting:

Engage Non-Converters: Use retargeting ads to reach users who have interacted with your content or visited your website but haven't yet converted.

Remind and Convert: Retargeting helps keep your brand top-of-mind and can lead to higher conversion rates.

Case Studies of Successful Paid Advertising Campaigns

Analyzing successful paid advertising campaigns can provide insights into effective strategies and tactics.

1. Case Study: Shopify's Facebook Ad Campaign:

Campaign: Shopify used Facebook ads to promote their ecommerce platform, targeting small business owners and entrepreneurs.

Outcome: By using engaging video content and precise targeting, Shopify achieved a significant increase in sign-ups and conversions.

2. Case Study: Airbnb's Instagram Ad Campaign:

Campaign: Airbnb ran an Instagram ad campaign showcasing beautiful travel destinations and user-generated content.

Outcome: The visually appealing ads and strong CTAs led to higher engagement rates and increased bookings through the platform.

3. Case Study: Chipotle's TikTok Challenge:

Campaign: Chipotle launched the #GuacDance challenge on TikTok to celebrate National Avocado Day.

Outcome: The campaign went viral, generating millions of video submissions and significantly boosting brand awareness and engagement on TikTok.

Paid advertising is a powerful tool for accelerating your social media growth. By understanding the unique advertising options on each platform, creating compelling and targeted ads, and maximizing your ROI through careful planning and monitoring, you can effectively increase your follower count and achieve your social media goals. Integrating paid advertising into your overall strategy can provide the boost you need to reach a million followers on Facebook, Twitter, TikTok, and Instagram.

Implementing these tactics, you can enhance your visibility, attract new followers, and achieve significant growth, complementing your organic efforts.

8

Leveraging Trends and Viral Content

Leveraging Trends and Viral Content

Introduction

Trends and viral content can dramatically increase your social media following. By staying current with popular topics and creating content that resonates with a broad audience, you can enhance your visibility and engagement. This chapter will explore how to identify and leverage trends, create viral content, and measure the impact of these efforts on your follower growth.

Identifying Trends on Social Media

Staying ahead of trends involves continuous monitoring and quick adaptation. Here's how to identify trends effectively:

1. Monitor Popular Hashtags and Keywords:

Hashtag Research: Use tools like Hashtagify, RiteTag, or the platform's search function to find trending hashtags.

Keyword Tracking: Track popular keywords related to your niche using tools like Google Trends or social listening platforms.

2. Follow Influencers and Industry Leaders:

Engage with Thought Leaders: Follow influencers and thought leaders in your industry to stay updated on emerging trends.

Join Industry Groups: Participate in relevant groups on Facebook, LinkedIn, and other platforms to gain insights into trending topics.

3. Utilize Trend Discovery Tools:

Social Media Platforms: Use built-in tools like Twitter's Trending section, Instagram's Explore page, and TikTok's Discover tab to find current trends.

Third-Party Tools: Platforms like BuzzSumo, TrendHunter, and Exploding Topics can help you discover trending content and topics.

4. Observe Audience Behavior:

Engagement Patterns: Pay attention to what your audience is engaging with the most. This can provide clues about trends within your specific community.

Creating Viral Content

Viral content has the potential to exponentially increase your reach and follower count. Here are strategies to create content that has a high potential to go viral:

1. Understand Your Audience:

Know Their Preferences: Create content that resonates with your audience's interests, values, and emotions.

Solve Problems: Content that addresses common problems or provides valuable information is more likely to be shared.

2. Emotional Appeal:

Trigger Emotions: Content that evokes strong emotions (joy, surprise, anger, awe) is more likely to be shared.

Tell Stories: Storytelling is a powerful way to connect with your audience on an emotional level.

3. Use Eye-Catching Visuals:

High-Quality Media: Use high-quality images, videos, and graphics to capture attention.

Attention-Grabbing Thumbnails: For videos, create compelling thumbnails that entice viewers to click.

4. Keep It Short and Simple:

Concise Messaging: Deliver your message quickly and clearly. Shorter content is more likely to be consumed and shared.

Easy to Share: Make it easy for users to share your content by including social sharing buttons and CTAs.

5. Capitalize on Trends:

Timely Content: Create content around current trends, events, or challenges. Being timely increases the relevance and shareability of your content.

Hashtags and Challenges: Participate in trending hashtags and challenges to increase visibility.

6. Encourage User Participation:

Contests and Challenges: Host contests and challenges that encourage user-generated content. This not only increases engagement but also expands your reach as participants share their entries.

Interactive Content: Use polls, quizzes, and questions to engage your audience and encourage sharing.

Measuring the Impact of Viral Content

To understand the effectiveness of your viral content, you need to measure its impact on your social media growth.

1. Track Engagement Metrics:

Likes, Comments, Shares: Monitor the number of likes, comments, and shares your content receives. High engagement indicates that your content resonates with your audience.

Reach and Impressions: Measure the reach (number of unique users who see your content) and impressions (total views of your content) to understand its visibility.

2. Analyze Follower Growth:

New Followers: Track the number of new followers gained during and after the viral content campaign.

Follower Demographics: Analyze the demographics of new followers to understand if you're reaching your target audience.

3. Monitor Website Traffic:

Referral Traffic: Use tools like Google Analytics to track the traffic to your website from social media. Viral content often drives significant referral traffic.

Conversions: Measure the number of conversions (e.g., sign-ups, purchases) generated from the viral content.

4. Assess Audience Sentiment:

Sentiment Analysis: Use social listening tools to analyze the sentiment of comments and mentions related to your viral content. Positive sentiment indicates successful engagement.

Case Studies of Successful Viral Campaigns

Examining successful viral campaigns can provide insights and inspiration for your own efforts.

1. Case Study: ALS Ice Bucket Challenge:

Campaign: The ALS Ice Bucket Challenge encouraged participants to dump a bucket of ice water over their heads and challenge others to do the same, raising awareness and funds for ALS research.

Outcome: The campaign went viral, generating millions of social media posts and raising over $115 million for ALS research.

2. Case Study: #ShareACoke by Coca-Cola:

Campaign: Coca-Cola replaced its logo with popular names on its bottles and encouraged people to share a Coke with friends and family.

Outcome: The campaign generated significant social media engagement, with users sharing photos of personalized Coke bottles, leading to increased brand visibility and sales.

3. Case Study: TikTok's #FlipTheSwitch Challenge:

Campaign: The #FlipTheSwitch challenge involved participants switching outfits and roles to the tune of Drake's song "Nonstop."

Outcome: The challenge went viral, with millions of users, including celebrities, participating and sharing their videos, significantly boosting TikTok's user engagement and visibility.

Leveraging trends and creating viral content are powerful strategies for rapidly increasing your social media following. By staying current with trends, crafting emotionally resonant and visually appealing content, and measuring the impact of your efforts, you can maximize your reach and engagement. These strategies, when combined with other growth tactics, can help you achieve your goal of reaching a million followers on Facebook, Twitter, TikTok, and Instagram.

Implementing these strategies, you can enhance your visibility, attract new followers, and keep your audience engaged, significantly contributing to your overall growth efforts.

9

Engaging with Your Community

Engaging with Your Community

Introduction

Building and maintaining a strong, engaged community is crucial for sustained social media growth. Engaging with your community not only fosters loyalty but also encourages word-of-mouth promotion, increasing your follower count organically. This chapter will explore strategies for effectively engaging with your audience, creating a sense of community, and handling feedback and criticism constructively.

The Importance of Community Engagement

Engaging with your community offers numerous benefits:

1. Loyalty and Trust: Regular interaction builds a sense of loyalty and trust among your followers.

2. Increased Visibility: Engaged followers are more likely to share your content, increasing your visibility.

3. Valuable Feedback: Interaction with your audience provides valuable insights into their preferences and needs.

4. Stronger Relationships: Building strong relationships with your audience can turn followers into advocates for your brand.

Strategies for Effective Community Engagement

To effectively engage with your community, consider implementing the following strategies:

1. Consistent Interaction:

Respond to Comments: Regularly respond to comments on your posts to show that you value your followers' input.

Like and Share: Acknowledge positive comments and user-generated content by liking and sharing them.

2. Host Q&A Sessions:

Live Sessions: Host live Q&A sessions on Facebook, Instagram, or TikTok to interact with your audience in real time.

Scheduled Posts: Create posts inviting followers to ask questions and provide thoughtful responses.

3. Create Polls and Surveys:

Engage Opinions:Use polls and surveys to gather opinions and preferences from your audience.

Content Ideas: Use the feedback to create content that resonates with your followers.

4. User-Generated Content (UGC):

Encourage UGC: Prompt your followers to create and share content related to your brand.

Feature UGC: Regularly feature user-generated content on your profile, giving credit to the creators.

5. Personalize Interactions:

Use Names: Address followers by their names when responding to comments or messages.

Personal Messages: Send personalized messages to thank followers for their support or to celebrate milestones.

6. Community Building Activities:

Host Contests and Giveaways: Run contests and giveaways to encourage participation and reward your followers.

Create Challenges: Launch challenges that encourage followers to create and share content related to your brand.

7.Exclusive Content:

Behind-the-Scenes: Share behind-the-scenes content to give your audience a glimpse into your process.

Early Access: Offer your community early access to new products or content as a reward for their loyalty.

Handling Feedback and Criticism

Constructive handling of feedback and criticism is essential for maintaining a positive community environment.

1. Listen and Acknowledge:

Active Listening: Pay attention to feedback and show that you value your followers' opinions.

Acknowledge Concerns: Publicly acknowledge valid concerns and thank followers for their feedback.

2. Respond Professionally:

Stay Calm: Respond to criticism calmly and professionally, avoiding defensive or confrontational language.

Provide Solutions: Offer solutions or corrective actions to address the issues raised by followers.

3. Learn from Criticism:

Reflect: Reflect on the feedback and consider if there are areas where you can improve.

Implement Changes: Make necessary changes based on constructive criticism to enhance your community's experience.

4. Encourage Positive Interactions:

Moderate Comments: Moderate your comments section to ensure a positive and respectful environment.

Highlight Positivity: Highlight positive interactions and contributions from your followers.

Examples of Effective Community Engagement

Examining examples of successful community engagement can provide inspiration and practical insights.

1. Example: Starbucks' Engagement Strategy:

Community Involvement: Starbucks frequently engages with its community through social media by asking for feedback on new products and sharing user-generated content.

Outcome: This approach has built a loyal community of followers who actively engage with the brand and promote it organically.

2. Example: Glossier's Customer-Centric Approach:

Customer Interaction: Glossier engages with its community by responding to comments, featuring customer stories, and incorporating feedback into product development.

Outcome: The brand's commitment to customer engagement has fostered a strong, loyal community that feels valued and heard.

3. Example: Wendy's Twitter Engagement:

Humorous Interactions: Wendy's has gained a large following on Twitter by engaging with its community through humorous and witty interactions.

Outcome: This unique approach has increased the brand's visibility and created a highly engaged and loyal community.

Engaging with your community is essential for building a loyal and active follower base on social media. By consistently interacting with your audience, creating opportunities for participation, and handling feedback constructively, you can foster a positive and supportive community. This engagement not only strengthens your relationship with existing followers but also attracts new ones, contributing to your goal of reaching a million followers on Facebook, Twitter, TikTok, and Instagram.

—-

End of Chapter 9

This chapter highlights the impBy implementing the strategies outlined, you can build a strong, engaged community that supports your growth and enhances your presence across social media platforms.

10

Analyzing and Adjusting Your Strategy

Analyzing and Adjusting Your Strategy

Introduction

Regularly analyzing and adjusting your social media strategy is crucial for sustained growth and engagement. By assessing your performance, understanding what works, and making data-driven adjustments, you can continuously optimize your efforts and achieve your goal of reaching a million followers. This chapter will explore how to effectively analyze your social media performance, identify areas for improvement, and implement changes to enhance your strategy.

The Importance of Analysis and Adjustment

1. Performance Tracking: Regular analysis helps you track the effectiveness of your efforts and identify successful strategies.
2. Informed Decisions: Data-driven insights allow you to make informed decisions about your content and engagement strategies.
3. Continuous Improvement: By identifying and addressing weaknesses, you can continuously improve your social media presence.
4. Adaptability: The social media landscape is dynamic. Regular analysis helps you stay adaptable and responsive to changes.

Key Metrics to Analyze

Understanding which metrics to track is essential for effective analysis. Here are key metrics to focus on:

1. Follower Growth:

New Followers: Track the number of new followers gained over a specific period.

Unfollows: Monitor the number of unfollows to identify potential issues with your content or engagement.

2. Engagement Metrics:

Likes, Comments, Shares: Measure the level of interaction with your posts.

Engagement Rate: Calculate the engagement rate by dividing the total engagement by your number of followers.

3. Reach and Impressions:

Reach: The number of unique users who have seen your content.

Impressions: The total number of times your content has been viewed.

4. Content Performance:

Top-Performing Posts: Identify which posts receive the most engagement.

Content Types: Analyze the performance of different content types (e.g., images, videos, stories) to determine what resonates best with your audience.

5. Audience Demographics:

Demographic Data: Analyze the demographics of your audience, including age, gender, location, and interests.

Audience Growth: Monitor how your audience demographics change over time.

6. Website Traffic and Conversions:

Referral Traffic: Track the traffic to your website from social media platforms.

Conversion Rate: Measure the number of conversions (e.g., sign-ups, purchases) generated from social media traffic.

Tools for Social Media Analysis

Several tools can help you gather and analyze social media data:

1. Native Analytics Tools:

Facebook Insights: Provides data on page likes, post reach, engagement, and audience demographics.

Twitter Analytics: Offers insights into tweet performance, follower growth, and engagement metrics.

TikTok Analytics: Tracks video views, follower growth, and audience demographics.

Instagram Insights: Provides data on post reach, engagement, follower growth, and audience demographics.

2. Third-Party Tools:

Hootsuite: Offers comprehensive social media analytics and reporting.

Sprout Social: Provides in-depth performance analysis and audience insights.

Buffer: Offers analytics for engagement, reach, and follower growth.

Google Analytics: Tracks referral traffic and conversions from social media to your website.

Adjusting Your Strategy Based on Analysis

Once you've gathered and analyzed your data, it's time to adjust your strategy. Here's how:

1. Identify Patterns and Trends:

Analyze Data: Look for patterns and trends in your data to understand what works and what doesn't.

Spot Weaknesses: Identify areas where your performance is lacking and determine the underlying causes.

2. Optimize Content:

Content Types: Focus on creating more of the content types that perform well.

Posting Schedule: Adjust your posting schedule based on when your audience is most active.

Content Quality: Continuously improve the quality of your content based on feedback and engagement.

3. Refine Targeting:

Audience Segmentation: Use demographic data to refine your targeting and reach the right audience.

Custom Audiences: Create custom audiences for more precise targeting in your paid advertising campaigns.

4. Enhance Engagement:

Interactive Content: Increase the use of interactive content (e.g., polls, Q&A sessions) to boost engagement.

Community Building: Focus on building a strong, engaged community through regular interaction and user-generated content.

5. Experiment and Innovate:

A/B Testing: Continuously run A/B tests to compare different versions of your content and strategies.

Stay Updated: Keep up with social media trends and platform updates to stay ahead of the curve.

Examples of Strategy Adjustments

Real-world examples of successful strategy adjustments can provide valuable insights:

1. Example: Netflix's Social Media Strategy:

Original Strategy: Netflix initially focused on promoting new releases and announcements.

Adjustment: They shifted to a more engaging approach by creating memes, interactive content, and behind-the-scenes videos.

Outcome: This adjustment significantly increased engagement and follower growth across their social media platforms.

2. Example: Nike's Instagram Engagement:

Original Strategy: Nike primarily posted high-quality promotional images and videos.

Adjustment: They began incorporating user-generated content, athlete stories, and interactive posts.

Outcome: The enhanced engagement strategy resulted in higher interaction rates and a stronger community connection.

3. Example: Wendy's Twitter Strategy

Original Strategy: Wendy's used a traditional promotional approach on Twitter.

Adjustment: They adopted a witty and humorous tone, engaging directly with followers and other brands.

Outcome: This unique approach led to viral tweets, increased engagement, and substantial follower growth.

Conclusion

Regularly analyzing and adjusting your social media strategy is essential for continuous growth and engagement. By tracking key metrics, using the right tools, and making data-driven adjustments, you can optimize your efforts and achieve your goal of reaching a million followers. This iterative process ensures that your strategy remains effective and responsive to the dynamic social media landscape.

By implementing these practices, you can ensure that your strategy evolves with your audience and the ever-changing social media environment, leading to sustained success.

All Rights Reserved
Olivia Westwood
2024

www.ingramcontent.com/pod-product-compliance
Lightning Source LLC
Chambersburg PA
CBHW071944210526
45479CB00002B/807